How To Make Your Business Stand Out With A USP And Guarantee

John Millar

Copyright © 2016 John Millar

All rights reserved. No part of this publication may be reproduced, distributed, or transmitted in any form or by any means, including photocopying, recording, or other electronic or mechanical methods, without the prior written permission of the publisher, except in the case of brief quotations embodied in critical reviews and certain other noncommercial uses permitted by copyright law

All rights reserved.

ISBN: 1540555062
ISBN-13: 9781540555069

DEDICATION

I dedicate this book to my mother and father, who raised me while self-employed. They
taught me to work hard and listen to everyone but to make my own choices as to what is right
and what is wrong.. and oh, did I mention work hard?

Anyone who tells you to work smart not hard hasn't ever done it tough and realized that if
you work smart AND hard you will achieve more than you can possibly dream.

JOHN MILLAR

CONTENTS

How To Create Your USP	8
USP ASA BUILDER	9
Creating a Powerful Guarantee	87
USP & Guarantee Questionnaire	95
About the Author	112
Testimonials	114

How To Create Your "Unique Selling Proposition" (Usp)

That Makes Your Marketing Generate More Results

Boost Your Sales And Profits By Positioning Your Company As The Best Choice In The Market

What makes you more unique, more valuable, and more visible in the market? You've heard the old saying "Differentiate or Die" right? In our highly competitive world, you have to be unique and fill a special niche to be successful in the marketplace. Yet one of the most harmful mistakes small businesses make is not being unique and positioning themselves as the best choice in the market. How do you show that your product or service is the best?

Use a Unique Selling Proposition or "USP". Having a USP will dramatically improve the positioning and marketability of your company and products by accomplishing 3 things for you:

1. Unique - It clearly sets you apart from your competition, positioning you the more logical choice.

2. Selling - It persuades another to exchange money for a product or service.

3. Proposition - It is a proposal or offer suggested for acceptance.

The Force That Drives Your Business And Sales Success

Your USP is the force that drives your business and

success. It can also be used as a "branding" tool that deploys strategy with every tactical marketing effort you use, such as an ad, a postcard, or web site. This allows you to build a lasting reputation while you're making sales. The ultimate goal of your USP and marketing is to have people say to you... *"Oh, yes I've heard of you. You're the company who..."* - And then respond by requesting more information or purchasing.

The Federal Express Example:

Federal Express (FedEx) dominated the package shipping market with the following USP: "Federal Express: When it absolutely, positively has to be there overnight." The deployment of this USP allowed Federal Express to emerge as the dominant leader in the industry, taking market share rapidly, and also increasing its sales and profits.

In today's competitive market, your business cannot thrive if you are using the same old "me too" marketing that everyone else is using. Your small business absolutely positively has to have a USP that "cuts through the clutter", separates you from the competition, and positions you as the best choice... the ONLY choice.

Building your USP takes some effort, but it is absolutely worth it because of the added advantage you'll have in the market. Using a powerful USP will make your job of marketing and selling much easier, enabling you to more easily increase your sales and profits for the same budget.

Winning USP Examples

The following are 6 powerful USPs that alleviates the "pain" experienced by the consumers in their industries..

Example #1 - Package Shipping Industry

Pain - I have to get this package delivered quick!

USP - *"When it absolutely, positively has to be there overnight."* (Federal Express)

Example #2 - Food Industry

Pain - The kids are starving, but Mom and Dad are too tired to cook!

USP - *"Pizza delivered in 30 minutes or it's free."* (Dominos Pizza)

(This USP is worth $1 BILLION to Dominos Pizza)

Example #3 - Real Estate Industry

Pain - People want to sell their house fast without loosing money on the deal.

USP - *"Our 20 Step Marketing System Will Sell Your House In Less Than 45 Days At Full Market Value"*

Example #4 - Dental Industry

Pain - Many people don't like to go to the dentist because of the pain and long wait.

USP - *"We guarantee that you will have a comfortable experience and never have to wait more than 15 minutes or you will receive a free exam."*

Example #5 - Cold Medicine Industry

Pain - You are sick, feel terrible, and can't sleep.

USP - *"The nighttime, coughing, achy, sniffling, stuffy head, fever, so you can rest medicine."* (Nyquil)

Example #6 - Jewelry Industry

Pain - The market hates paying huge 300% markup for jewelry.

USP - *"Don't pay 300% markup to a traditional jeweler for inferior diamonds! We guarantee that your loose diamond will appraise for at least 200% of the purchase price, or we'll buy it back."*

How To Develop Your Unique Selling Proposition (USP)

Your USP is the very essence of what you are offering. Your USP needs to be so compelling that it can be used as a headline that sells your product or service. Therefore, since you want to optimize all your marketing materials for maximum results, create it before anything else (such as advertisements and marketing copy).

Print this article and jot down your ideas to construct a "Unique Selling Proposition" (USP) for your business. Follow this easy 7-step process:

Step 1: Use Your Biggest Benefits:

Clearly describe the 3 biggest benefits of owning your product or service. Let me be blunt. Your prospect doesn't care if you offer the best quality, service, or price. You have to explain exactly WHY that is important to them. Think in terms of what your business does for your customer and the end-result they desire for a product or service like yours. So, what are the 3 biggest benefits you offer? Write them down on a piece of paper...

1.
2.
3.

Step 2: Be Unique:

The key here is to be unique. Basically, your USP separates you from the competition, sets up a "buying criteria" that illustrates your company is the most logical choice, and makes your product or service the "gotta have" item. (Not your competitor's.)

Write your USP so it creates desire and urgency. Your USP can be stated in your product itself, in your offer, or in your guarantee:

- PRODUCT: "A unique baseball swing that will instantly force you to hit like a pro."

- OFFER: "You can learn this simple technique that makes you hit like a pro in just 10 minutes of batting practice."

- GUARANTEE: "If you don't hit like a pro baseball player the first time you use this new swing, we'll refund your money."

Write your ideas on paper now...

Step 3: Solve An Industry "Pain Point" Or "Performance Gap":

Identify which needs are going unfulfilled within either your industry or your local market. The need or "gap" that exists between the current situation and the desired objectives is sometimes termed a "performance gap". Many businesses that base their USP on industry performance gaps are successful.

For example, Domino's Pizza used the "Pizza delivered in 30 minutes or it's free" USP to become wildly successful. This worked because of the need or "gap" in the market
- After a long day at work Mom and Dad are too tired to cook. But the kids are starving and don't want to wait an hour! They want pizza NOW. Call Domino's.

So, what are the most frustrating things your customer experiences when working with you or your industry in general? Alleviate that "PAIN" in your USP and make sure you deliver on your promises. Write your ideas on paper now...

Step 4: Be Specific And Offer Proof:

Consumers are skeptical of advertising claims companies make. So alleviate their skepticism by being specific and offering proof when possible. Write your ideas on paper now...

Step 5: Condense Into One Clear And Concise Sentence:

The most powerful USPs are so perfectly written, you cannot change or move even a single word. Each word earns you money by selling your product or service. After you get your USP written, your advertising and marketing copy will practically write itself!

Now take all the details about your product/service/offer from the steps above and sculpt them into one clear and concise sentence with compelling salesmanship fused into every single word. Write your ideas on paper now...

Step 6: Integrate Your USP Into ALL Marketing Materials:

Variations of your USP will be included in the ALL your marketing materials such as your...
- Advertising and sales copy headlines;
- Business cards, brochures, flyers, & signs;
- Your "elevator pitch", phone, and sales scripts;
- Letterhead, letters, & postcards;
- Website & Internet marketing.

Step 7: Deliver On Your USP's Promise

Be bold when developing your USP but be careful to ensure that you can deliver. Your USP should have promises and guarantees that capture your audience's attention and compels them to respond to you. Having a strong USP can make your business a big success, or a big failure if you don't deliver on it thereby ruining your reputation. In the beginning, it was a challenge for

Federal Express to absolutely, positively deliver overnight, but they developed the system that allowed them to deliver the promise consistently.

Conclusion:

Using a powerful USP is the driving force that builds your business success. Build your USP and use it to optimize your marketing materials for maximum results.

USP ASA BUILDER

This part of the book has been designed to give you Information and Inspiration to help you create a Unique Selling Proposition for your business, product or service.

Becoming The Obvious Choice In A Sea Of Competition

There is no choice; YOU MUST READ THIS ENTIRE DOCUMENT. Take notes, underline key points, highlight any BFO's (Blinding Flash of the Obvious) and then most important of all TAKE ACTION. The future of your business may depend on it.

Don't tell them what you do. Tell them what you do for them.

As a business owner, service provider or even medical

professional, one of the biggest challenges you will face is telling others what you do. The challenge comes from the fact that most people are only interested if what you do fits what they need or want. Otherwise they are not interested. You must tell the listener how your product or service can benefit him, and how you can do it better than others who do what you do.

Differentiation, niche marketing, and positioning. These and other related business buzzwords have no doubt crossed every business owner and marketing director's ears in recent years.

But what do these words *really* mean to **you** in **your** business? Usually they mean that a business will attempt to sell a product or service that is somehow different than the competition's to a certain, specific target market. In theory, this is a great idea. If you could just reach that one segment of the market with your great, new, innovative product...

Welcome to reality. If your company is innovative enough to develop a truly unique product or service that is earning you a profit, the following inevitably happens: competition springs up from nowhere to imitate your product or service, undersell your price, and steal your market share. It's immutable.

So, as your next line of defense, you choose to position yourself as the **quality** leader within your field. Or as the **low price** leader. Or as the **service** king. You soon find yourself in a battle with four other companies – all claiming to have the largest selection, lowest prices, highest quality or best service.

A marketing free-for-all usually ensues. Each competitor tries in vain to shout with the loudest voice that his business is superior. Headlines get bigger, radio ads get more obnoxious, advertising agencies get richer. More significantly, **customers begin to discount any claim made by any of the companies.**

Is niche marketing the way to go then? Obviously, different is better than "me too." The question isn't whether or not to be different, but rather *how to communicate those differences* in a way that your customers will <u>believe and embrace them</u>. **Your Real Opportunity for Innovation Lies in the Marketing.**

Here's What Marketing Really Is...

You need to realize three things about business to understand marketing. These three things are always true, *regardless of what industry you're in:* **1)** All businesses do just one thing: **They Woo Customers** – Period. **2)** All customers want just one thing: **The Best Deal** – Period. **3)** Your marketing should do just one thing: **Articulate Why You're The Best Deal** – Period. You can build confidence if you **articulate** your advantage.

This is not a complicated thing. If you dispute any of the three points, please call me to discuss it at once. I don't want to be wrong about such simple stuff. But if this is such simple stuff...then *why do most businesses have so much trouble executing a decent marketing plan?* I say it's because, in general, **we are lazy communicators**.

See if this scenario sounds familiar. When you get home

from work, your spouse asks you how your day was. What do you usually say? Fine, okay, I'm tired, great, it stunk. Do these words actually communicate anything? What about when you see someone you know at the store and you ask, "Whatcha doin'?" (as if you really care or can't tell by looking) and he answers, "Fine," which is actually the answer to the other question he was expecting, which is *"How ya doin'*?" We are a society of lazy communicators...**we are on communication autopilot**. Don't think, just talk.

These communication habits spill over into marketing and advertising all the time. Show me 99% of all marketing material created and I'll show you a huge jumble of hyperbole, fluff, platitudes, and yawnably unbelievable, black hole nothing words. Words like cheapest, professionalism, service, quality, speedy, convenient, and best. These words do absolutely nothing to communicate **why you're the best deal**. NOTHING. Claude Hopkins, the greatest advertising man in history, summed it up: *"**Platitudes and generalities roll off the human understanding like water from a duck. They leave no impression whatsoever**."*

Firstly, let's look at what some Marketing experts have called an ASA (Articulated Sales Argument)

The most powerful tool you can use to stand head and shoulders above your competition is the Articulated Sales Argument (ASA). Your ASA is the singular, unique benefit that your customers can expect to receive when they favor your business instead of your competitor's – stated in specific, graphically illustrated terms.

In a nutshell, the ASA is the argument you build, the case you design, and the reasons you give why a prospect should do business with you. Your ASA should distinguish your business from all the competitors. It will make you the obvious choice and lead prospects to the conclusion, **"I would have to be an absolute fool to do business with anyone but you...regardless of price."**

You may have associated the ASA to current business buzzwords like "niche marketing" or "unique selling proposition." The difference is we are not only going to introduce you to the concept, we are going **to help you** implement the underlying principle in a systematic way in your business.

An ASA Will Raise Your Business Above The NOISE

Take a look in the yellow pages and you will find pages of ads for nearly every given product or service. Each ad seems to shout the same thing: "best, cheapest, honest, friendly service" and many other empty words. We call this condition NOISE and it is one of the primary reasons for the Confidence Gap. This condition is not exclusive to the yellow pages, it is in every aspect of marketing and advertising. How then can a prospect determine which, if any, of the offers is the greatest deal? Generally speaking, they cannot. The result is a prospect calling the first few ads then going with the lowest price.

You may be aware that in your industry lowest price does not always reflect the best deal. You can probably name a competitor or two that offer a lower price than you. You can probably also identify how buying from your competition would result in less value for the same money spent. The most important question is **does your marketing make your value clear to the prospect?**

Build a Case For Your Product Or Service Like An Attorney Would

Envision your marketing situation as a court case - your prospects are the jury, you are the defendant and you must prove to them without a doubt that your product or service is the most practical alternative amidst all the competition. Now remember: this is a life or death situation. Under these circumstances, are you going to settle with a defense that says, "we're better, we're cheaper, we're professional or we've got better service"? Of course not! You are going to probe your jury to know what they will be sympathetic to and respond to. You are going to give substantial, quantifiable evidence to back yourself up.

Once you have gathered this information about your business or developed your ASA, selling becomes incredibly easy. You will have the entire framework for any marketing and media you will ever need to create for your business. In effect, you have defined the "Inside Reality" or the "something good to say." Once you have this clearly defined, you are ready to work on the "Outside Perception" or "saying it well."

Here's an example of an ASA in action.

An air conditioning repair company in Las Vegas harnessed the power of the ASA and tripled the size of its business in less than a year. Before developing and implementing an ASA, the company had been guilty of running "me too" advertising. Their yellow pages ad (where 90% of their business came from) had the company name plastered across the top in huge letters. Bullet points let everyone know that they provided 24-hour service, they serviced most major brands, they had 22 years of experience, etc.

Because everyone else's ad said essentially the same thing and since their ad was relatively large, they were able to build a respectable business in spite of their "me too" approach. Each year, they were able to generate enough revenue to do the following:

1) Add a new truck or two to their fleet.
2) Keep their repairmen busy most of the time.
3) Generate a small profit for the owners.
4) Continue to run the advertisement.

What more could small business owners ask for? A lot more! The first step in developing their ASA was to determine what customers wanted most from an air conditioning repair company. In the 8 month long Las Vegas summer even a couple of hours without an air conditioner is sheer misery. <u>Customer surveys</u> confirmed their notion – fast service was to be the premise for their ASA.

But everyone else already claimed to have fast service. Some companies even put FAST SERVICE in big headlines at the top of their ads. It wasn't as if nobody else had ever figured out that being fast was important. The funny thing was that nobody else had ever figured out a way to **say it in a way that would allow them to stand head and shoulders above the competition.**

The next year they ran a half page ad as usual (no additional expense), but changed the wording to say, "Because we have 58 repairmen on call 24 hours a day to man our 27 service trucks, we can guarantee that your home or business will be cool within 2 hours of your call – or there's no charge for the repair." **And that was just the headline!**

The rest of the ad went on to explain that if the crews were too busy to fix the unit right then or if the repair would take longer than 2 hours, portable units would be brought in to cool the house at no extra charge until the repair was completed. Bottom line, the customer would be cool in a hurry – period.

The company put a lot of faith in their new ASA based on previous test results – they actually only had 17 repair trucks and about 40 technicians when they first placed the ad. They were counting on the ad to generate enough business to afford them the additional trucks and personnel. The number of calls the ad generated *quadrupled* in less than one month after the new book came out. More importantly, they were able to convert 50% of the calls into jobs – up from 38% before. Gross revenues soared and new trucks were bought to keep up with demand. The end of the year profit for the owners was higher than they thought they would ever see.

Their integration of the ASA "fast service" was the key element in the company's turnaround. Obviously, other factors contributed as well, like the company's underlying dedication to fulfilling the "big promise" of fast service. But the point is a simple headline stating the ASA "fast service" increased their bottom line by over 400% with **no additional advertising cost.**

What's Your ASA?

The ASA really is the keystone of all your marketing. Everything else depends on it.

Another name for ASA is the Unique Selling Proposition or USP

Every day, you're inundated with more than 1,500 advertising messages. If you're like most people, you're spending huge amounts of energy just trying to block out those messages.

Now, turn this issue around and ask yourself: "How do I get my message across when most people are trying hard to dismiss it?" The answer is in your USP — your Unique Selling Proposition.

The concept of "USP" is credited to Rosser Reeves, chairman of the Ted Bates & Co. advertising agency in the 1950s. He was one of the first to develop a technique for communicating in an overcrowded marketplace. His definition of what makes a USP holds true today:

- All advertising must make a proposition to the customer: Buy this, and you will receive a specified benefit.
- The proposition must be unique; something competitors cannot claim, or have not chosen to emphasize in their promotions.

- The proposition must be so compelling that it motivates individuals to act.

The concept of USP has evolved since Reeves' groundbreaking work, but it remains a foundation of successful marketing. USP is nearly synonymous with positioning, and is integrally related to branding strategy. These concepts share a common focus — making a specific offering unique and desirable to a specific audience.

A unique selling proposition (USP) is a succinct, memorable message that identifies the unique benefits that are derived from using your product or service as opposed to a competitor's. A USP should be used as a strong and consistent part of an advertising campaign. It can be painted on the company's cars or trucks, printed on the letterhead, and used in the packaging copy. It becomes, essentially, a positioning statement—a declaration of your company's unique standing within the marketplace as defined by your product's benefits.

Often a USP is a quick and snappy condensation of the

company's strategy. This is especially true when a company offers one type of product or service. But even more so than most strategies, USPs tend to focus on one or two of the most powerful and easily communicated benefits derived from using a product or service.

The USP might focus on price, quality, dependability, breadth or depth of the product or service line, technical edge, fashion, customization, specialization, or nature of service.

Your unique selling proposition is the core of your marketing message. It tells suspects, prospects and customers about the value you provide in a clear, concise format. It is not a job description – "I wash windows" but a statement of purpose with a benefit – **"I improve your view of the world outside your window."**

To build long-term product recognition, a business owner/advertiser or marketing agency should focus on getting consumers to remember one succinct and consistent message regarding its product. To expect consumers to remember a continually changing or drawn-out message is a near-futile hope.

It is particularly important that a USP immediately convey one of the strongest competitive advantages of using your product. Otherwise you are simply engaging in trade association-type advertising or, in other words, promoting all products within your marketplace or industry.

Marketers should strive to create a significant perception of difference between their product and the offerings of competitors. This becomes particularly important, and of course a more difficult job, when competitive products or services have virtually identical features that offer like benefits. Developing a USP that accomplishes this task is called product differentiation.

For example, a perfume manufacturer could use the product name, packaging, and advertising to create a certain distinct mood or feeling about each of its product lines. It can carefully target each line to a specific audience.

Think of Shalimar—"The Gardens of Shalimar have inspired thousands of lovers. And one perfume." Or Liz Claiborne's Vivid—"A spirit that will not be denied."

Similarly, a cola bottler or brewer of beer may use a USP to identify its product with a fun and appealing lifestyle that creates a positive product differentiation.

Great examples of effective product differentiation include Wal-Mart's "Always the low price," FedEx's "Absolutely, positively overnight," UPS's "We run the tightest ship in the shipping business," Stouffer's "Nothing comes closer to home," or Midas Muffler's "Guaranteed for as long as you own your car."

Here's an example of an effective USP from a well-known company - the biggest in their field - in an extremely competitive industry. This company became the biggest in their field entirely because of their USP. The company is Domino's Pizza. Consider Domino's USP:

"Fresh, hot pizza delivered to your door in 30 minutes or less, guaranteed!"

This USP built Domino's into a pizza empire!

Let's look at what made Domino's USP successful?

First, it specifically answers the question of why should I do business with them. The answer, of course is, call them if I want **fresh, hot pizza delivered to my door in 30 minutes, guaranteed.**

Secondly, this USP is very specific and meaningful. It doesn't say "it'll be there soon." Or, "it will be delicious." It says only that you will get fresh, hot pizza delivered in **30 minutes, guaranteed!**

You can imitate Domino's Pizza's USP to create a USP for your own business. You just need to think about how your business answers the question listed above.

Another aspect of an effective USP is that when you tell someone your USP, it should prompt the following response:

"Really? How do you do that?"

Say you're at a party and someone asks you what you do. Instead of telling them your title or what you do, tell them your USP. If you tell them, "I'm an automotive recycler," that person is merely going to nod and smile.

On the other hand . . . lets say your USP is:

"I save business owners thousands of dollars each year by _____."

Or...

"I give _____ that shows any business how they are almost always blowing thousands of dollars a year on _____."

Or...

"I am a _____expert who shows companies how to add extra profits to their bottom line by teaching them how to save money on their _____ costs."

Or...

"In 15 minutes, I show people how to save hundreds, even thousands of dollars on _____ they regularly overpay for."

Or...

"I show businesses who spend $x,xxx a year on _____ how to protect themselves from being overcharged."

With these USPs, there's a good chance a prospect will ask you, "Really, how do you do that?" You then tell them about how your business can save them money.

Why it works

USP works because of a simple fact of cognitive behavior. One of the ways the human mind handles the barrage of advertising it receives is to pick something to believe, then hold that notion until forced to change.

Snap judgments become permanent beliefs, since it is uncomfortable and difficult to change convictions once formed. The mind tends to filter out new information that doesn't support already held beliefs. This attribute of the mind, called "anchoring," explains why USP is an effective strategy.

Areas to consider when developing YOUR USP/ASA

Target Market/Specific Group

To understand what will be compelling to your target market, you must know what these consumers value. Study what they buy, and how they make their purchase decisions. Consider your potential customers in terms of their demographics, lifestyle and purchase characteristics.

Your goal is to match the benefit you promote to the needs and issues customers care about.

The best USP statements are personalized to the group or individual you are addressing. For example, when speaking to a doctor, I would say

"I help medical professionals find more profitable candidates for their elective procedures."

When speaking to a diverse group (such as the chamber of commerce) I would be more general:

"Ace Communications designs hair-on- fire marketing programs that help you attract more clients and earn more money."

Knowing your target market will also enable you to communicate better with them. So let's get specific. Here are some guidelines: Page 127 Instant Leads Bradley J. Sugars

Age: How old are they?

Sex: Are they male, female or both?

Income: How much do they earn?

Where do they live: Are they local, or do they come from miles around to deal with you?

Competitors

Since it's often better to be first than best, it's important to know what beliefs the target market now holds about you and about your competitors. What might research tell you? Remember that competition can come from direct or indirect sources. For example, while all publishers of how-to books are direct competitors to the Dummies books, indirect competition also comes into play from how-to courses and seminars.

It is difficult and expensive to challenge a competitor for a position already occupied, because of the "anchoring" phenomenon. When you know your competitors' positions, you can choose to avoid direct challenges and instead carve out your own niche, where you can be both first and best.

Study your competition. Search online for potential competitors. Pick the top 5 to 10 and try to determine their USP. Most will not have a clear USP, for these look for some of the features or services that they stress.

Now look for the gap in their products or services. What area of the market is not being serviced?

Positioning

Better to be first. The easiest way into a person's memory is to be first. In the mind, second is not a unique position — it's merely the start of "the rest of the pack." The mind can remember some levels beyond "first" and "other," but divisions quickly become fuzzy among the also-rans.

Because of the "anchoring" tendency, being first is better, even if being first is not logically important. Consider the explosion of self-help books with titles like "XYZ for Dummies," "Complete Idiot's Guide to XYZ," "Beginner's XYZ," and so on.

The first entrant, the "Dummies" series, now holds more than two-thirds of the market for self-help books. The other publishers were later entrants, and so they struggle to gain a share of the remaining market.

There is no logical reason to believe a "Dummies" book contains more useful advice for novices than other books intended for the same audience. Still, two out of three of us cast our lot with the "Dummies."

Developing your USP is the art of choosing and communicating a dimension in which you can make a compelling claim to be first — and therefore, in the marvelously illogical mind, best.

But what is "positioning" and how can you use it? Some examples:

SONY has been first at innovation. They want to be first in whatever's next in technology.

K-Mart is the cheapest store, they won't be undersold.

Low price and full lines are their battlefields for your mind.

"What's the best battlefield (Strategic Position) for you to take?"

You must understand that any decision to buy from, or use a company's services, first takes place in the mind of the customer. If your company, products, or services are not in their mind, they probably won't use you. **You basically, "aren't there" without a position.**

Some of the most common examples of positioning are service, speed of delivery, latest technologies, guarantees, and lowest price.

Your company has probably already carved out a niche for itself. But, if you're like most business owners, you probably haven't identified what your niche is. Usually it's the salespeople and customers who know the niche better than the owners do.

When it comes down to it, customers are the ones who

really know a company's niche best. You can use the 80/20 rule to do some research about your company. The 80/20 rule is that 80% of a company's profit comes from 20% of their customers. Find out who the "20%" of your best customers are. Find out why they are doing business with you instead of someone else. This will tell you where your **real niche** or **core competency** is. If you think you do one thing and your best customers think you do another thing, you need to make a decision. What causes this difference in perception? Did your marketing do a better job of advertising your weaknesses than your strengths? Did you accidentally advertise what you do least instead of best?

If from your results you think you're marketing the wrong USP and losing business because your market has the wrong perception of you, then change it!

These are not minor decisions for you and your company to make. These can be "make-it or break-it" decisions. The good thing is you can survey your market. Track the results of sales and make necessary changes. These decisions are critical to building a HIGH-PROFIT business.

You have to communicate any changes to your market. A well stated USP is the way to accomplish this.

Getting Into The Minds Of Your Prospects

So, how do you get into your prospects' minds?

You find or create your own position and communicate it over and over again to the right target market.

Here is something you must keep in mind when marketing your company, (almost no one does):

You have to be perceived by the public as being different from your competition!

Your prospects have to see you as having something different, something special that sets you apart from the others in your industry. Otherwise, there's no reason for them to call you. They may call your competition or they may decide not to call anyone at all.

To the general public everybody in your industry may seem all the same. You know that's not true. Good positioning finds and communicates what's different about you. What sets you apart from others that do the same work as you do. Determine what makes you unique, what your differences are, so the uninformed public will know how they will benefit by doing business with you.

Now, the next thing in determining your strategic position is to discover and communicate the following things:

· Who you are
· What you do
· Why you're different
· How you can benefit your prospects

There should be a lot of differences between you and others doing the same kind of work. If there aren't then you're not paying close enough attention or you need to invent some unique things that others don't do.

Some examples might be:

· Open weekends and evenings

· Special financing options

· New breakthrough equipment

· No premium for after-hours work

· Family owned for 25 years

· Specializing in _____

· Great guarantees

· Something for FREE (that perhaps the rest of the industry charges for)

Benefits

Before a purchase is likely to happen, a magical act of transformation must take place: Features must be turned into benefits. A feature is anything you have designed into the product or service. A benefit is what the customer gets out of it. A feature may be useful, but it is not of compelling interest in and of itself. A benefit is a solution to a problem, a fulfillment of a desire.

Take a camping lantern with a head-mounting strap. You designed the head-mounting strap into the product; that's a feature. The customer gets hands-free operation of the lantern; that's a benefit.

Even if you can't find a completely unique feature to promote, search for one that other competitors have overlooked. When you find it, you've got the "U" for your USP.

Tell your prospect how you can ease his pain. This presupposes that you understand the problems of your target market, and have a solution.

Some people get this backward, and create a solution in search of a problem (or create a problem in search of more problems!).

People will not use you unless they are going to get some kind of benefit. You have to clearly and succinctly tell and show them how they will benefit by doing business with you.

Benefits do <u>not</u> include things like:

· We really care

· Locally owned and operated

· Friendly service

These things don't really say what you'll do for someone. They are vague and unspecific.

Some examples of benefits might be:

· We guarantee to save money on your _____ costs

· Deadline promises kept or we pay you — guaranteed

· We guarantee you'll get same day quotes

After you come up with as many benefits as possible, ask some of your customers what benefits they have gotten from your relationship.

In trying to list the benefits of doing business with their company, many owners end up with a list of *features* instead of *benefits*. Just remember a feature is an item or facet of your product or service. A benefit is what that feature will DO for someone.

You need to see what people get out of buying your products or services. What do they end up with when it's all said and done? Do you ever get compliments/comments from your customers? How can you translate those into benefits? Keep your focus. Really see things from the eyes of your customers. You not only have to listen to what they say about you being unique and how you uniquely solve their problems, but you should also use the language they would use to describe that uniqueness.

It is vitally important that you know the benefits you can give prospects and to be able to communicate this to them. When you speak to prospects or customers you must speak in customer language. You must have the view point of the consumer and talk in terms the consumer understands. Think of it this way. If your best customer were to tell someone else why they do business with you, what would they say?

Differentiate

How is your business (and you) better and different than who you compete with?

What does this mean? I want you to list all the ways that you think you are better than others in your industry. What do you feel your strengths are? Very few can be good at all things and if you were, no one would believe you anyway. But for now, list all the ways you think you are better. Keep in mind here you are going to want to tell your prospects how you are different from others in your profession without bad-mouthing or slamming the other guy.

If you start saying, "and I've done this and I've done that and I've done the next thing ... I can do all these things for you," pretty soon you're the jack of all trades. Jack of all trades and expert of none is what your market will think.

Look at if from your public's view point:

· Are there ways you give better service than others?

· Are you more experienced in certain areas?

· Are you more personal?

· Do you have better guarantees or better payment options?

· Do you have better equipment?

You might think that it's too much work to create your USP. Believe me, it's not if you want a profitable business. The only reason your public is uninformed about the benefits of doing business with you is because YOU haven't informed them.

Most USPs fall into one of 10 main categories.

These 10 categories are:

1. **Low Price**

   Guaranteeing the lowest price has been used as a USP for many online merchants. Unfortunately many who have chosen this for a USP are no longer in business. Doing business online does have some cost and overhead advantages over off-line business and most online customers do expect some of these savings to be passed on in the form of discounts.

   However, cutting profit margins too deeply is rarely healthy for a business or market. If your company is small, you run the risk of setting off a price war or angering the larger players in your market, who due to economies of scale, can afford to match or beat your prices short term to force you out of the market, long term.

There are of course many examples of businesses that have adopted this USP and survived or even prospered. The philosophy is low margins but high volume. The best example of successful implementation of this USP is Wal-Mart.

Wal-Mart's USP statement is short, sweet and to the point. **Wal-Mart – "Always Low Prices. Always"**

2. High Quality

The high quality USP is based on a high margin, lower volume philosophy. This USP is often found hand in hand with other USPs such as "Superior Service" and "Strongest Guarantee".

One brand that immediately comes to mind

when you think about quality is Rolex. While there are actually watches that cost more than a Rolex, the general public immediately recognizes a Rolex as a high quality timepiece.

Rolex also has a short USP statement that communicates volumes.
Rolex – "Quality Takes Time"

3. Superior Service

In today's marketplace unless you want to position yourself simply as a "Lowest Price" commodity, you have to add value. Providing superior customer service is a wonderful way to add value as well as develop long-term customer loyalty.

Good customer service should be and is expected. What I am talking about here is the "above and beyond" type of customer service. I frequently console my clients to go beyond just satisfying their customers. You have to AMAZE them.

A good example of a company that has adopted "Superior Service" as their USP is <u>Rackspace</u> Managed Hosting. In a very crowded market of "Lowest Price" competitors, Rackspace has managed to differentiate itself very successfully by focusing on giving extra mile service. I host several of my higher traffic sites on Rackspace dedicated servers and have found their staff to be knowledgeable and helpful.

Rackspace sums up their USP statement in two words. **<u>Rackspace</u> – "Fanatical Support"**

4. **Size/Selection**

Being the "biggest" in your market or providing the largest selection of items in your niche can be a powerfully effective USP.

The classic example of this is Amazon.com.

Were they the first online bookstore? While many people think that they were, there were actually several companies selling books online before Amazon.com. Are they the lowest price? Nope. While their prices on books are low, if you look around enough you can find them cheaper elsewhere online. So what made Amazon.com blow away other companies that entered the market sooner or had thousands of retail stores? Selection. For years Amazon's USP was **"Earth's Biggest Bookstore."**

Even though they were not the first and today they have intense competition from all of the "brick and mortar" stores such as

Barnes and Noble, Borders and B. Dalton, who have set up their own websites, Amazon.com still leads the pack in online bookselling because they clearly differentiated themselves early on by being "Earths Biggest Bookstore." This clear USP was the reason for their rapid growth and early success.

While they have changed their current USP to be a bit diluted and broad, Amazon.com's original USP was clear and focused.

Amazon.com – "Earth's Biggest Bookstore."

5. **Convenience**

The "convenience" USP is based on centering your business around your customers needs. By removing as many obstacles to ordering, receiving or using your product or service as possible, you are placing the customers convenience at the centre of your business model.

A good example of the "Convenience" USP is Schwan's. This company has been delivering frozen food items to customer's homes for over 50 years. They have kept up with technological changes by adding the convenience of online ordering and multiple payment options.

Schwan's USP statement sums up their commitment to customer ease and convenience.

Schwan's – "Shopping should be easy. Cooking should be fun."

6. **Knowledgeable Advice, Recognized Authority**

This USP works well for professionals and other skill or service based organizations.

This USP says "I am the top in my field. You can trust my knowledge and experience."

You have probably seen the wild infomercials for Mathew Lesko's "Government Grants and Giveaways" book. Mr. Lesko, through his wild and crazy antics has positioned himself as a leading authority on taking advantage of government waste and special interest programs.

His USP statement makes his claim to be the leading expert in his specialty.

Matthew Lesko – "America's Leading Expert on Free Government Money."

7. Customization/Most Options

Giving your customers more options or custom building your products to their individual specifications works.

One company that made a name for itself by using customization as it's USP is Ping Golf Clubs. Ping was the first company to custom fit golf clubs to the swing of each individual player. This was a revolutionary concept in the 1960's. This unique approach to club building has made Ping one of the most recognized and respected names in golf.

Ping's USP statement reflects their commitment to custom fitting their products to their customer's needs.

Ping – "The leaders in custom fit, custom built golf clubs."

8. Speed

The speed at which your product or service is delivered can be a powerful USP in today's fast paced environment. Offering Overnight or 2nd Day Air shipping as a standard service in a niche or market that is used to standard ground shipping can give you a strong competitive advantage. It was not too long ago that the standard for shipping in mail order was 4 to 6 weeks. (Remember those days?)

Federal Express revolutionized the industry when it began guaranteeing overnight delivery of packages.

The FedEx USP statement explains exactly why to use their service.

FedEx – "When It Absolutely Has To Be There Overnight."

9. Originality, First in Marketplace

Sometimes your product is so new and unique that the product itself is the USP. Unfortunately in today's competitive environment this type of USP is short lived.

Before too long a competitor will emerge with a knock-off or copy of your product.

However, until then promote the newness and uniqueness of your product as the USP. When the competition heats up switch your USP focus to being the "original" or "first". Being the original or first mover in the market is a USP that nobody can duplicate.

An online example of this is OilOnline.com. Since they were established in 1995 dozens of other sites have popped up targeting the oil industry, however OilOnline.com has maintained its dominant position in this market by using its claim to being the first site to target this niche.

OilOnline.com's USP statement emphasizes their "first mover" status in their niche.

OilOnline.com – "The Original Online Source for the Oil Industry."

10. Strongest Guarantee

Most customers assume that a company will stand behind their product or service, but a clear, strong guarantee turns the assumed into the assured. But with the level of competition out there today, you need to make your guarantee stand out from the crowd. This is an area that you can differentiate yourself from your competition. Make your guarantee so strong that when compared to your competition's, your customer would be crazy to go elsewhere.

Craftsman tools are a prime example of this USP. Craftsman claims that, "If any Craftsman hand tool fails to provide complete satisfaction, return it for free repair or replacement. Period. The first Craftsman hand tool we sold back in 1927 is still under warranty today." Now that's a strong guarantee.

Like all well thought out USPs, the Craftsman USP statement leaves no doubt what their main advantage is.

Craftsman Tools – "Hand tools so tough, they're guaranteed forever."

More home grown examples to keep you focused.

Hungry Jacks "the burgers are better at Hungry Jacks"

Dick Smith Power House "It starts with Low prices and just gets better"

KMART "Cutting the cost of living"

Bunnings "Lowest Prices are just the beginning" Tell me, what's their Guarantee…….

Pedders Suspension "Expert service and advice you can trust and No Bull"

Avis "We're No 2 we try harder"

Mitre 10/10 on everything

Challenged?

Consider these strategies for uncovering your unique benefit, your USP, your ASA.

1. **Against a competitor or category.**
   Remember the rental car giants Avis vs. Hertz? Avis' "We're No. 2. We try harder" turned a disadvantage into a memorable emphasis on service. When soft-drink leaders Coke and Seven-Up butted heads, Seven-Up promoted its "Un-cola" status to set itself apart from the whole category of cola beverages.

2. **Reposition the competition.** Make your competition the villain, rather than the benchmark of good performance. When Tylenol took on conventional aspirin, it did so with ads that proclaimed, "Aspirin can irritate the stomach lining.... Fortunately, there is Tylenol."

3. **Focus on the problem.** All photocopiers do pretty much the same thing — make copies. But the latest technological enhancement is an internal modem that can place a service call, even if the copier is unattended when it breaks down. Dealers for the enhanced copier stand out from their competitors by focusing on the problem of downtime.

4. **Better value.** When other products deliver the same benefit as your offering,

then something other than product features must set yours apart as the better value. Your convenient location, or extended warranty, or free home delivery, or lower price point may be your USP.

5. **Users and usage.** If the "80/20" rule of thumb holds true, it's likely that 80% of your business comes from the 20% who are your best customers. What are these people like? Dramatize their loyalty to your offering, and you will attract others like them. Consider using a high-profile spokesperson from this group of loyalists to get your message across.

6. **Examine you own business.** Sit down and brainstorm with your staff possible USP concepts. Don't judge the ideas, just write

them down. To stimulate thought and ideas ask the following questions:

- What do we do the best?
- What do we do better than our competition?
- What awards have we won?
- What have our customers said about us?
- What praise do we often get from our customers?
- What endorsements for celebrities or well know organizations do we have? What endorsements could we get?
- What does our product or services do better than anyone else?
- How is our business model different

from our competition? How could it be different?

- What market category or niche is not being served by our industry?

- What is unique about your business or brand vs. direct competitors? You'll probably find a whole list of things that set you apart; the next questions will help you decide which of these to focus on.

- Which of these factors are most important to the buyers and end users of your business or brand?

- Which of these factors are not easily imitated by competitors?

- Which of these factors can be easily communicated and understood by buyers or end users?

- Can you construct a memorable message (USP) of these unique, meaningful qualities about your business or brand?

- Finally, how will you communicate this message (USP) to buyers and end users? Marketing tools to communicate USPs include media advertising, promotion programs (e.g., direct mail), packaging, and sales personnel.

It is also helpful at this stage to interview and survey your current and past customers. Ask them why they bought from you rather than your competition? What are they looking for in a provider of your product or service? What is important to them when making a buying decision? What feature or benefits do they value most or would like to see added to your product or service?

7. **Use the USP Questionnaire provided at the very last part of this book.** (A very obvious choice)

NOW's the time for ACTION

Actions USP questionnaire is an excellent way to start the creative juices flowing. It gives you a launching pad and it provides a simple process of revealing the hidden potential every business has, their Unique Selling Proposition.

Or you can begin to write down and crystallize your ideas. Don't worry about length at first, just write down the key points of your USP concept. Focus on the benefits to your customer of each concept. Develop a list of 5 to 10 possible USPs.

Show this list to your staff, friends, family and current customers. Get their input and suggestions and use these suggestions and comments to narrow your USP concept down to a single main differentiating concept.

Once you have settled on the most unique and compelling feature of your product or business, begin to distill it down to one paragraph that clearly communicates and sums up why your customers should buy from you. This paragraph can be used on your website or in your marketing materials where you have more room to explain the unique benefits that you bring to your customers. However, it is still too long to be used as a tag-line or slogan.

You still need to distill your USP down to one or two focused sentences that clearly and concisely communicate the benefits of your USP to your customers. This statement should leave no question in your customers mind about what you do and how you are different than your competition.

This USP statement will become your tagline or

slogan. This process will take some time and your USP statement may require several revisions before you are comfortable with the final draft.

Integrate your USP statement into everything you do. Put it on every page of your website, on your letterhead, in all of your advertising and marketing. Communicate it to your employees, managers and staff. Let it infuse into your corporate culture. Every time you talk to your customers, employees or suppliers you should mention this USP. You cannot just give lip service to your USP, you have to live it and breath it! It must become a part of you.

Every product, business or service has (or can have) a USP that makes it stand out from the competition. It is up to you to discover or create this element of uniqueness. Differentiate yourself, your business and your products from your competition and watch the sales pour in!

Let's make this Absolutely Clear. There are some

major benefits to spending quality time and energy in developing your USP/ASA….naturally **INCREASED PROFITS is one of them.**

Focus: Keeps your team pointed in the right direction and focuses your group on delivering the promise.

Advantage: Tells your customer what the specific advantage your organization has over the competition.

Image: Creates a persuasive image for your customer of what you will do for them.

Reason: Gives a distinctive reason for the customer to buy from you.

Differentiates: Your business in the eyes of your current and potential customers or clients.

Still finding it a challenge, then maybe your USP is one of the following:

- ✓ You offer the cheapest price for the product or service you're selling, than any other company.
- ✓ You offer a higher quality product or service than any of your competitors.
- ✓ You offer the widest choice or selection of products than anyone else.
- ✓ You provide more customer service, assistance or education, before, during and after the sale than any of your competitors.
- ✓ You offer more bonus products, services or premiums than anyone else.
- ✓ You offer the fastest delivery time for your products than any of your competitors.

You offer a longer period of guarantee or warranty than any of your competitors.

In case you think that I have been somewhat repetitive in this document, you're absolutely correct. And just to make sure you have understood the importance of developing a USP/ASA for your business, product or service, I have added just a little more information and inspiration.

"Your USP is Like A Maverick 'Pick-Up Line' That Will Have Customers Favoring You Over Everyone Else"

Remember that a USP is a marketing concept invented by Rosser Reeves in the 1960's. Reeves, who wrote *Reality in Advertising*, came to the conclusion that the only way to make customers come to you was to create an advertising message about your product that contained the following three characteristics:

1. Each advertisement must make a proposition to the consumer. Not just words, not just product puffery, not just show-window advertising. Each advertisement must say to each reader: "Buy this product, and you will get this specific benefit."

2. The proposition must be one that the competitor

either cannot, or does not offer. It must be unique--either a uniqueness of the brand or a claim not otherwise made in that particular field of advertising.

3. The proposition must be so strong that it can move the mass millions, i.e. pull over new customers to your product.

Reeves used this idea to create unique selling propositions for many consumer products such as Anacin ("The pain relievers doctors recommend most"), M&M candies ("They melt in your mouth, not in your hands"), Colgate ("Cleans your breath while it cleans your teeth"), and Wonder Bread ("Helps build bodies in eight ways"). With the USP, he built those products and companies into billion dollar giants.

The strategy of creating and then sticking to a USP is as powerful today as it was then, and is still used by savvy marketers to build million dollar and billion dollar firms. If you have the right type of USP for your product or service, that type of outcome is not out of reach.

Since that time, the idea of the USP, also known as a unique buying advantage, has slowly expanded beyond its original bounds. Borrowing some of the findings of Doug Hall, we now also know that successful USPs should have the following characteristics:

- A Big, Overt Promise of BENEFITS for customers who buy the product or service
- A REAL REASON to BELIEVE that the benefits claim is credible and that customers can TRUST that those promised benefits will actually be delivered
- A DRAMATIC DIFFERENCE to those promised benefits that makes the offering unique and distinguishes the product or service apart from its competitors

- It should be short, simple, memorable, attention getting, persuasive, motivating and compelling just by its WORDING alone
- The USP should be an ECONOMICALLY FEASIBLE idea that can sustain a business for at least 5 years or more
- It should absolutely penetrate the business, by operational design and outward appearance, to lend overall guidance to the idea of customer service and managerial alignment throughout a firm

Federal Express created one of the most famous USPs of all time when it said: "When it absolutely, positively has to be there overnight." When Fred Smith founded Federal Express, there was no such thing as an airfreight package delivery service that could reliably deliver packages overnight in a consistent fashion. Everyone knows FedEx now, but the business of Federal Express is not so much the package delivery business as it is the business of delivering peace of mind. FedEx's customers fear late delivery, so FedEx composed a unique selling proposition that focused on delivering the peace of mind that the package would get there on time.

FedEx grew into the international, multibillion dollar giant it is today because of both its business design and its simple USP that it trumpeted over and over again in its advertising: "When it absolutely, positively has to be there overnight." FedEx so organized its business structure and strategies, hiring, training, tracking capabilities, management rewards, uniforms, corporate communications, delivery methods and facilities ALL around the single promise of making overnight deliveries without fail. FedEx became focused on delivering upon that USP which they had determined was the most attractive one for the package delivery market. FedEx is organized (aligned) around that promised benefit.

Anyone can readily recognize that this USP

promises the benefit of overnight delivery for customers. But the real genius of this USP escapes most people, which is the fact that it subtly offers a real credibility for that promise through the words, "positively, absolutely." Without those words, Federal Express's service promise would lose its punch and believability. Those two words telegraph that this company means what it says ... it means business ... you WILL get your package delivered tomorrow.

Domino's Pizza, on the other hand, also grew into a super successful national franchise despite having literally thousands of local competitors all across the country - largely because of a simple business model and a simple USP that also greatly differentiated it from all its competitors. Domino's promised the pizza customer an experience that was rare in the pizza home delivery market. Its USP was "Hot, fresh pizza delivered in 30 minutes or less, guaranteed."

Let's say that one again: "Hot, fresh pizza delivered in 30 minutes or less, guaranteed."

Before Domino's Pizza, your chances of ordering and then promptly receiving a "fresh and hot" pizza were "slim to none" since it usually arrived cold, late, and sticking to the top of its box. Definitely there was room for better pizza service. Dominos knew this, so they came out with their famous unique selling proposition - a true customer buying advantage - and they went national by sticking to their word. If you didn't get your hot pizza on time, you didn't have to pay and so the company organized itself around the promise of fast delivery.

Because most people already knew what pizza tasted like, Dominos didn't promise a tasty pizza or lots of tomato sauce or extra toppings. Dominos stuck to impressing you with one major promise … fast, reliable delivery of a hot pizza.

What was the believability factor to get over the pizza credibility hump? To make its USP believable and entice customers to give them a try, Dominos offered a guarantee. They promised that if your pizza didn't arrive at your door within 30 minutes, you'd get it for free. That one factor differentiated it from everyone else and enabled it to cream all its competition. Other pizza companies now focus on different USPs (Papa John's trumpets, "Better ingredients, better pizza) while Little Caesars promises two pizzas for the price of one), but you can see how powerful a simple idea can be in creating billion dollar monsters.

Yes, USPs can take you to become a millionaire and then billionaire, if you hit it right!

What are you waiting for... begin the journey of more sales and increased profits TODAY.

USP ASA BUILDER

What Should You Guarantee? – Creating a Powerful Guarantee

Again, the easiest way to get started here is to answer a few questions, just to get you thinking. To come up with a powerful guarantee, you need to know what your customers want you to guarantee, and what you actually can promise.

The idea is to match your abilities with your customers' wants. Often, it's a good idea to over promise. You probably underrate your product or service anyway. If you think it's good, why not promise that it will be great - it'll make you pick up your act, and probably be more in line with your current customers' perceptions anyway.

Here are the questions...

What is your current guarantee?

Creating a Powerful Guarantee

What are 3 problems or frustrations buying your product/service solves?

1.
2.
3.

What frustrations do customers experience when trying to find your product or service?

What frustrations do customers experience when they go to buy your product or service?

What are the 3 major benefits of buying your product or service?

1.

2.

3.

What frustrations do customers experience when using your product or service?

Creating a Powerful Guarantee

What frustrations do customers experience after they've bought your product or service (e.g. - lack of after-sales service)?

If you were a customer, why would you dislike buying from you?

Describe the sort of potential customers who love buying from you ... and why?

If you could easily overcome any 2 of your customers frustrations what would they be and how would you overcome them?

1.

2.

3.

What 6 things that will relieve your customer's frustrations that you can guarantee, and deliver 100% of the time right now?

1.

2.

3.

Creating a Powerful Guarantee

4. ....

5. ....

6. ....

What 3 additional things will you be able to fully guarantee within the next 3 months?

1. ....

2. ....

3. ....

List 3 things that you can NOT confidently guarantee today, that you would love to be able to guarantee tomorrow ...

1.

2.

3.

What is the ONE thing that, if you could guarantee it, would make you the market leader? (For example, a news agency that guarantees to sell you a winning lottery ticket every time). Is there any way in the world, within the realms of human possibility, that you could offer this; even it backfired some of the time?

Creating a Powerful Guarantee

USP & Guarantee Questionnaire

Your Competitors

First, let's take a look at the other businesses in your industry...

List your 3 biggest competitors...

1.

2.

3.

What do they do well?

1.

2.

3.

What do they do poorly?

1.

2.

3.

What would the average person say about each of these competitors?

1.

2.

3.

What is 'unique' about them?

1.

2.

3.

What 'Guarantees' do they have in place?

1.

2.

3.

How are these guarantees promoted?

1.

2.

3.

How 'genuine' are these guarantees?

1.

2.

3.

What can't each of your competitors guarantee?

1.

2.

3.

What can they do that you can't?

1.

2.

3.

Where are they geographically located in comparison to you and your potential market place?

1.

2.

3.

Your Industry

Describe how your industry has changed in the last 5

years...

Describe the changes you expect to see in the next 12 months in your industry...

Describe the changes you expect to see in the next 5 years in your industry...

Tell us about any regulations on marketing in your industry...

Describe the perceived standards of customer service in your industry...

Describe the perceived standards of technology in your industry...

Describe the perceived standards of product quality in your industry...

Describe the perceived standards in sales & marketing in your industry...

How does your business compare to these industry standards?

- Customer Service?
- Technology?
- Product Quality?
- Sales & Marketing

What are businesses in your industry required to guarantee?

Your Ideal Scenario...

List 3 things that you cannot confidently guarantee today, that you would love to be able to guarantee...

What is the one thing that if you could guarantee it, would make you the market leader? (For example, a newsagent that guarantees to sell you a winning lottery ticket every time?)...

In an ideal world, what would you like your customers to see as the main point of difference between you and your competitors?

If there were one phrase your customers and prospects used to describe what you do now, it would be...
'Oh, you're the guys who...'

If there were one phrase your customers and prospects used to describe what you do in an ideal world it would be...
'Oh, you're the guys who...'

Think of 3 industries as far removed from yours as you can, then from each one, 'steal' an idea that could give your business a real point of difference (for example KFC - Finger licking good.)

Industry 1...
Industry 2...
Industry 3...

Your Market Place...

Describe who the average customer is for your

industry...

How old is the typical customer? (Circle the approximate age groups)

Under 15   20   25   30   35   40   45   50   55   60   65   Over

What percentage of your potential market is (avoid putting 50/50)...

Male ....%   Female.................%

What is most important to an average customer in your industry? (Rank in order, from 1 being most important, to 10 being least important). Also circle the one you think is most important.

Quality		Speed of service	
Price	....	Customer Service	....
Reliability	....	Consistency	....
Safety	....	Back up Service	....
Convenience	....	Image	....
Guarantee	....	Other	....

Is the current market place growing or diminishing? Please explain.

In dollar terms, how much money is spent in your industry each year in your geographically serviceable market place?

Is your typical customer different from the generic industry customer you have described?

Your Specific Niche...

Describe your current average customer...

Describe your ideal future customer...
Rank the priorities of your ideal future customer in the same way as you ranked the priorities of your generic industry customer. Pay particular attention to the differences, if any...

Quality   Speed of service
....

Price	Customer Service	
Reliability	Consistency	
Safety	Back up Service	
Convenience	Image	
Guarantee	Other	

What are 4 reasons your customers come to you rather than your competitors? This question is particularly important, so give it some real thought.

1.

2.

3.

4.

In what 4 ways do you perceive that you are genuinely different from your competitors?

Below are some 'niches'. Fill in where your competitors fill a niche. For example, Volvo is known for safety, Porsche for speed.

1.   Quality   _____

2.   Speed of service   _____

3. Price   _____
4. Customer Service _____
5. Reliability   _____
6. Consistency   _____
7. Safety   _____
8. Back up Service _____
9. Convenience   _____
10. Image   _____
11. Guarantee   _____
12. Other   _____

Based on the above, which niche do you believe you fill?

What can you do that no one else can?

Claude Hopkins, advertising guru, made a beer company the market leader with one ad… all he did was describe the process the company went through when making the beer. Please describe in detail how your product is made and delivered…

What are the 5 things about your product or service

that you take for granted, that your customers don't know about?

1.

2.

3.

4.

5.

Your Customer's Thoughts...

What are 3 things your best customers say about you?

1.

2.

3.

What are 3 things your worst customers say about you?

1.

2.

3.

What would an average customer have said about you 12 months ago?

How would their opinion differ now?

Below you'll see 4 questions to reproduce on a Customer Feedback Form... So that we can both get the best possible understanding of your customers' perceptions, copy it and get 8 of your customers to complete it during the next week ... This questionnaire has been designed to be easily and quickly answered by our customers - it also makes them feel they are helping to improve your service.

This information helps us to understand your business from your customers' perspective, and it will help you to accurately measure the feeling of your market place. Simply run through the questions with 8 of your customers this week...

Once you have completed the Feedback Forms, go on to the next question...

Having now completed the Customer Feedback exercise, how do you feel, and what have you learnt?

Customer Feedback Form Questions

1. What are the three major reasons you buy from us and not somebody else?
2. What is the point of difference that makes you want to deal with us?
3. If you could improve 2 things about us, what would they be, and how would you change them?
4. What are the 2 things that annoy you the most when dealing with businesses in our industry?

Your Customers' Frustrations...

What are 3 problems or frustrations that buying your product/service solves?

1.
2.
3.

What are the 3 major benefits of buying your product or service?

Creating a Powerful Guarantee

1.

2.

3.

What frustrations do customers experience when trying to find your product or service?

What frustrations do customers experience when making a decision whether or not to buy your product or service?

What frustrations do customers experience when they go to buy your product or service?

What frustrations do customers experience when receiving or picking up your product or service?

What frustrations do customers experience when using your product or service?

What frustrations do customers experience after they've bought your product or service?

If you were a customer, why would you dislike buying from you?

Describe the sort of customers who dislike buying from you... and tell us why?

Describe the sort of customers who love buying from you... and tell us why?

If you could easily overcome any 2 of your customers' frustrations, what would they be and how would you overcome them?

1.

2.

Your Past and Present...

What is your current written guarantee?

How is this different from your guarantees of the past?

How do customers react to your current guarantee?

What have you learnt from the changes that you have make to your guarantee to date?

If you have one, what is your current marketing positioning statement? (ie. It's Mac time now, or Always Coca-Cola.)...

How is this different from your past attempts

How do customers react to your current positioning statement?

What have you learnt from the changes that you have made to your positioning statement to date?

What You CAN Guarantee...

What 6 things will relieve your customers' frustrations that you can guarantee and deliver 100% of the time right now?
1.

2.

3.

4.

5.

6.

What 3 additional things will you be able to fully guarantee within the next 3 months?

1.

2.

3.

ABOUT THE AUTHOR

John Millar is the Managing Director, Senior Business Coach Trainer and Consultant with More Profit Less Time Pty Ltd and CEO-ONDEMAND. Along with his many other business interests, John is proud to have been an associate of the most successful coaching team in the world.

He is recognized as a global leader and has been benchmarked against over 1,300 colleagues in 31 countries. John has over 25 years of hands-on ownership, management, coaching, and entrepreneurial experience in a broad range of industry sectors, including retail, wholesale, import, export, IT, trades and trade services, automotive, primary production, food services, transport, manufacturing, mining, professional services, the fitness industry, and more.

He has extensive experience developing and providing training for small to medium-sized companies and a variety of publicly listed corporate companies. John is an accomplished and talented public and professional speaker. He has been a mentor working with sales/management activities for businesses with a turnover under $100,000 per annum, over $100 million turnover, and everything in between, with great success.

John currently works with business owners and their teams across Australia and has a "Whatever it takes" attitude that has enabled him to help his clients grow their business profits by up to 800%.

If you are ready to be coached by one of the best in the business, register at:

www.ceo-ondemand.com.au

Make sure to visit www.moreprofitlesstime.com for

the new online Management Development Program: The Business Essentials Series.

CEOONDEMAND

ACCLAIM FOR JOHN MILLAR'S

Business Coaching and Training in their own words...

"Without John Millar as my Business Coach I wouldn't have a business today."—Grant Jennings Managing Director, Jigsaw Projects

"Taking the decision to be coached and trained by John Millar was carefully considered after experiencing those who over promised and under delivered. I am pleased to say the content of his courses are the tools we all need to master as business owners. His delivery is engaging, thought provoking and empowering and after every session I came away re-energised. John always makes himself available for business building advice both via Skype and face to face beyond the scope of delivery. With his extensive personal experience in building small businesses, he knows and understands what it takes to establish and grow a business. I have no hesitation endorsing John Millar as an educator and business coach and the bonus is he is a very nice person." —Anne Lederman Managing Director FB Salons"

Johns training with my management team was excellent, it was very different from the business coaching and support I have had in the past. John was clear, thoughtful and he addressed the issues we needed to cover without us even knowing they were being addressed! His follow up has been fantastic and exactly what I needed. I would recommend John and his team to anyone looking at getting some business coaching and training done" —Wendy Crawford, Peopleworx

"In my dealings with John as our business coach, I have found him to be a motivated and insightful agent of positive change. He is able to burrow down to the root cause of issues and introduce effective forms of measurement. John then identifies and implements practical solutions and is there to provide the gentle persuasion required to ensure that results are achieved." —Mark Felton, Lindale Insurances

"You have coached and trained us so well throughout the year that we are now used to & find it easy to prepare a 90 day plan, then breaks it down to actionable bite size pieces. Planning in business & personal life certainly is important. It allows us to identify the important things & the bigger picture. Thank you for your support & guidance throughout the year. And not to mention your insight, external perspective to review & assist our business moving forward." —Linda Turner, Director Roy A McDonald Certified Practicing Accountants

"If you want to achieve sales results you never thought were possible and give yourself a competitive edge my strong suggestion is to engage John services and listen closely to what John has to say, during the time I was trained by John I was one of eight sales consultants in a national business for 10 out of the 13 months I lead the sales tally and in 1 quarter I generated three times the revenue of the national sales force combined. Johns training and experience was well worth the investment and paid big dividends. Thanks John." —Julian Fadini, Bellvue Capital

"John is a very enthusiastic trainer and business coach, he is very passionate about getting business owners and their team where they need to be. He goes the extra mile to keep ahead of the latest developments which he then uses to benefit his clients." —Darren Reddy CPA

"I have been to a few seminars and heard John speak numerous times about sales, marketing and business. He is a very knowledgeable and extremely enthusiastic business coach in all his interactions and I would recommend him to all business owners who need a sales and marketing boost!" —Andrew Heath, Managing Director, Fresh Living Group

"I worked with John Millar and found his business knowledge, passion and innovation to be inspiring. He has always been able to set (and achieve) strategic long and short-term goals both for himself and his clients without losing that personal connection he builds with everyone he meets. He has been and I believe will continue to be a strong mentor and trainer for anyone wanting to take that next step in their business." —Bree

Webster, Online Marketing Guru

"Massive Action Day" – what an understatement, John Millars 4 hour frenzy challenged me to seriously review areas of my business I would not have gone to .... In this way, the process identified incongruence's in my mind, my business and my modus operandi. It's created a paradigm shift. Thanks John, the road map just got a whole lot clearer. Your friendship and insights since 2003 have been a gift to my business and I." —Andrew Reay, Counsellor, Hypnotherapist and Counsellor, Thinkshift Transformations

"John Millar is not your usual Business coach or trainer; he gets involved with you and your business and provides hands on help to make sure you follow through on his advice. He is highly motivated to help his clients and his personal guarantee certainly shows this. He has now transposed his thoughts, advice and love of good business onto a series of DVD's in his business venture – More Profit Less Time. This has excellent tips and advice for anyone either starting out or already in business. I highly recommend John to any business owner who wants to run a business and not a j.o.b.!" — Darren Cassidy, Managing Director HR2U

"I and many of my Business Partners and colleagues have worked with John since 2010 as our business oath, trainer and motivator and found him to be an extremely motivational person to assist us achieve our business goals. This company and its products allows for John's skill set to be accessed by a wider number of potential clients. His very professional DVD series is extremely good value for money and is easily accessible for all of us who are time poor. If you are looking to maximise your and your business's results and to start achieving your goals and dreams, contact John; you won't look back!!" —Mark Cleland, Mortgage Choice

"John develops real relationships with the people he comes into contact with. He is pasionate about what he does. His DVD and group training series, is full of good ideas and process to make your business better. Knowing what to do and actually doing it are two different things. John is excellent at helping you get things done." —Carey Rudd, Sales Director, Online

Knowledge

"I have known John since 2004 and found him to be extremely knowledgably in both Sales and Business systems as a business coach without peer. John has provided me with business advice as well as personal coaching over the years, helping me with the running of my organisation. I'm impressed with John's DVD series where he has condensed a lot of the information in an easy to follow format that any business owner can use immediately. I wish he had released these DVDs earlier, as they are a goldmine of information, and practical how to that allow anyone to increase the profit in their business and get back valuable wasted time." —Steve Psaradellis, Managing Director, TEBA

"John's DVD and workbook delivery of his no-nonsense advice provides a low-cost option for those business owners looking to set and achieve goals that will increase profit. I found the conversational style of the DVD's easy to follow, whilst the requirement to pause the DVD and write down some action points ensured a level of commitment to the advice being provided." —

How To Make Your Business Stand Out With A USP And Guarantee

Mark Felton, Lindale Insurances

"I only met John briefly at a BNI meeting and knew instantly i need to hire him for my business as my business coach. His attitude towards work and how to improve my cash line had an instant effect on before, even before I finally hired him on an official basis. I found myself thinking "what would John do" and this was only after just meeting him. I cannot see my business expend and give me "More Profit Less Time" without John's expert direction and training. If you want to succeed in business life, you need John Millar, without him you're just kidding yourself " —Leslie Cachia, Managing Director, Letac Drafting

"I can highly recommend John Millar to any business owner who wants to grow his business. When I hear very positive feedback from colleagues who are skeptics by nature about John's ability and skills, I know John will help all those he comes in contact with. John comes with a selfless nature and the willingness to work inside a client's business to make it succeed. Rare indeed!" — Darren Cassidy, Managing Director, HR2U"I first met

John Millar in mid-2010 and have always found him to be of an honest and generous character that engenders an easy association with him. I love how easy he is to listen to and how passionate he is about his work and topics. John demonstrates a love for life and his work and I have no hesitation in recommending his services."
—Kathie M Thomas, Managing Director, VA

"I have listened to John speak on a number of occasions and find him a very knowledgeable speaker with a passion for what he does. I have also interacted with a number of his clients and they all tell me that he helps them achieve results in their business. If you are looking for business help John is a person you can trust." — Carey Rudd, Sales Director, Online Knowledge

"John knows his stuff, he knows how the get results, John has so many great ideas in building a business and helping business owners work less and make more money. John has released a DVD set on doing just that. I have watched the 1st one and it was great, very informative and easy to understand, I happily recommend John to anyone in need of help and guidance" —Frank Eramo, Proprietor, Dynotune

"I have known John only for a short time, however the impact that he has had on me, not just my business has helped me to visualise opportunities that I began to doubt my ability to realise. He is encouraging and at the same time challenging so that he can/you can, begin to see how to maximise the business potential, John calls it being an unreasonable friend, I call it being a mate. If you have any questions about the direction of your business, if you want to seem your bottom line improve not just turnover but real profit, if you want a person who will work with you then I strongly recommend that you engage him at your earliest convenience. John is the best thing that has happened to my business. I could tell you about the way he is on track to make 1/2 a million for me on his contacts alone, but that actually sells him short, he has become like my partner in business, and cares about my success as if it was his own, we will flourish because I took the step to employ his training to help me grow. If you get a chance to get him training you, don't wait like I did, get in as quickly as possible, his time is your business and if like me your business is to make money, then every day you don't have him on retainer you lose money." —Russell Summers, Managing Director, The Give Life Centre

"It's usually easy to be mediocre in business but it's impossible when you have John Millar training you. He has been my right hand since 2003!" —David Manser, CFO, Hydrosteer

"I now have a commercial, profitable business and now it's my choice when I work IN my business and when I work ON it and have had john helping me in business since 1988. I can't imagine not having John as a part of our business." —David Wall, Director, D&K Transport

"The work John has done since 2008 coaching and training our marketing team, administration and finance teams, buyers, store managers and staff nationally have been fantastic." —Ross Sudano, Director, Anaconda Adventure Stores

"John is a creative, professional, practical and committed business coach and trainer. His approach since we first met him in 1994 to working with a client team through the application of useful tools, information and anecdotes along with his easy going & easy to understand delivery sets him apart from other business coaches that I have used in the past." — Anthony Beasley, Director, The Astra Group

"I have worked with John Millar for the since 2004 and I didn't think it was possible to achieve what we have achieved together. His business coaching, training and services just get better and better!" —Terrance Chong, Managing Director, Echo Graphics and Printing

"John's business coaching, training and support has transformed our business across Australia and New Zealand since 2008."—Rose Vis, Managing Director, VIP Australia

"We first met John in 2005, he is AMAZING at sales, marketing, operations, logistics, finance training and so much more. Since engaging John as our business coach our business has exploded, our team are happy, our clients are raving about us and my husband and I now take at least 12 weeks holidays a year, EVERY year." — Shirley Du, Director, Goldline Technology

"It's the no nonsense results driven business coaching and training focus John bought to the table that had such a massive effect on our business." —David Runkel, Director, Tracomp Fabrication and Steel

"We started working with John in early 2010, within 90 days of working with and being trained by John Millar we had the biggest and most profitable month in our 15 year history. That's impressive." —Hugh Gilchrist, Managing Director, Australian Moulding Company

"If you don't have John as your business trainer you aren't meeting your business potential." —Don Robertson, Director, Medallion Electrical Services.

www.ingramcontent.com/pod-product-compliance
Lightning Source LLC
Chambersburg PA
CBHW070029210526
45170CB00012B/504